# HAGIA SOPHIA

Sabahattin Türkoğlu

## NET

**TURİSTİK YAYINLAR**
SANAYİ VE TİCARET A.Ş.

Published and distributed by:
**NET TURİSTİK YAYINLAR A.Ş.**

**Şifa Hamamı Sok. No. 18/2, 34400 Sultanahmet-İstanbul/Turkey**
**Tel: (90-212) 516 32 28 - 516 82 61  Fax: (90-212) 516 84 68**

**236. Sokak No.96/B Funda Apt., 35360 Hatay/İzmir/Turkey**
**Tel: (90-232) 228 78 51-250 69 22 Fax: (90-232) 250 22 73**

**Kışla Mah., 54. Sok., İlteray Apt., No.11/A-B, 07040 Antalya/Turkey**
**Tel: (90-242) 248 93 67 Fax: (90-242) 248 93 68**

**Eski Kayseri Cad., Dirikoçlar Apt. No.45, 50200 Nevşehir/Turkey**
**Tel: (90-384) 211 30 89 - 211 46 20 Fax: (90-384) 211 40 36**

Photographs: **Uğur Ayyıldız, Erem Çalıkoğlu,**
**Tahsin Aydoğmuş, Naci Keskin, Ali Konyalı**
Layout: **Not Ajans**
Typesetting: **AS & 64 Ltd. Şti.**
Colour Separation: **Mas Matbaacılık A.Ş.**
Printed in Turkey by: **Mas Matbaacılık A.Ş.**

**ISBN 975-479-049-3**

8th Edition, 1995

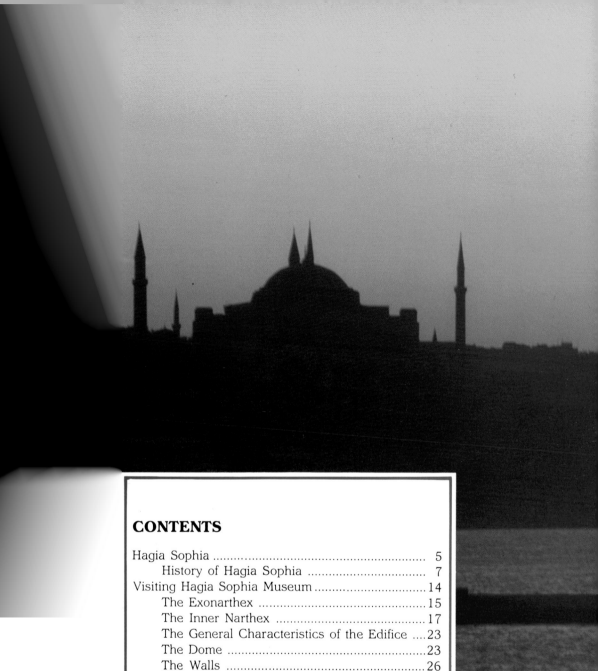

# CONTENTS

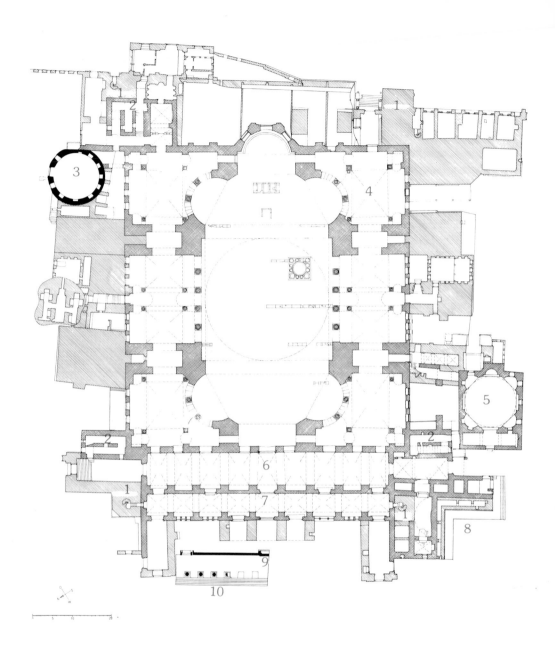

*Floor plan of the ground floor.*

1- Minaret
2- Staircase
3- Skevophylakion
4- Metatorium
5- Baptistery

6- Narthex
7- Vestibule
8- Remnants of the Patriarcal Palace
9- Remnants of the Atrium
10- Theodosian Vestibule

# HAGIA SOPHIA

One of the greatest monuments of Byzantium, Hagia Sophia was built in the 6th century, but its exterior does not exhibit the characteristics of that century. The buttresses built to support the outer walls to ensure their endurance over the centuries, and the changes made during the Turkish era, have markedly altered the outer appearance. Since it was used as a mosque for almost five hundred years after 1453, Islamic structures such as the minarets built on the corners of the main edifice, the fountain (şadırvan), mausoleum (türbe), and soup-kitchen (imaret) etc. give Hagia Sophia a mosque-like appearance. Consequently, 6th century architectural characteristics are much more apparent in the interior of the building.

In 1935 Hagia Sophia was converted into a museum, and it is now one of Turkey's two most popular museums. It is open every day except Mondays.

# HISTORY OF HAGIA SOPHIA

lthough there are no artifacts confirming it, it is said that Hagia Sophia was built on the site of an ancient pagan temple. Hagia Sophia underwent two phases of construction before attaining its present state.

Despite disparity of opinion, documents indicate that the first Hagia Sophia was built by Emperor Constantius, son of Emperor Constantinos I, and was opened for services in 360 AD. Although very little is known about this church, it is assumed that it was a basilica-type structure with a rectangular floor plan, circular apse and timbered roof. It was similar to St.Studios, a basilica in Istanbul, the ruins of which still exist. Ancient sources emphasize that the eastern wall was circular.

Constantius donated gold and silver as well as religious objects to his church, but these were vandalized by Arians during the Council of 381 AD.

*Reconstruction of the facade of the second Hagia Sophia.*

*Hagia Sophia was first named "Megale Ekklesia" (The Great Church) as it was the largest church in Constantinople. The historian Socrates indicated that the church was named Sophia during the reign of Emperor Constantius.The name given to the church symbolized the second divine attribute of the Holy Trinity. Originally, Sophia, which means "Holy Wisdom", was a name given to Christ by 4th century theologians.There is no connection with any saint. Both names, Megale Ekklesia and Hagia Sophia are used today.*

The original church was destroyed in 404 AD by mobs, during the riots started when Emperor Arcadius sent the Patriarch of Constantinople, John Chrysostom, into exile for his open criticism of the Empress.

Emperor Theodosius II built a new church which was completed in 415 AD. The architect of this second church was Ruffinos. The edifice was constructed in basilica-style and had five naves. In common with other basilicas of that age, it had a covered roof. The remains of this church, excavated in 1935, show that a staircase of five steps led to a columned propylaeum in front of the entrance of the building. Including the imperial entrance, there were three doorways in the facade. The results of excavations indicate that Hagia Sophia was 60 metres wide. The length is unknown, since further excavations inside the present-day edifice are not permitted.

In the fifth year of the reign of Emperor Justinian, on January 15th 532, Monophysites, discontented with the government policy and the rivalry between the Blue and Green parties in the hippodrome, rebelled. During the rebellion, Hagia Sophia was destroyed along with many other important buildings, among which were the Church of St. Eirene, Zorzip Bath and Samsun Hospital.

After resorting to bloodshed, Emperor Justinian succeeded in saving his throne. This revolt is known as the "Nike Revolt" in Byzantine history, since the rebels repeatedly shouted "Nike", the name of the goddess of victory.

Following these events, Emperor Justinian ordered the construction of a new church which was to surpass in magnificence all earlier churches. His ambition to make this new church unique, spurred him on to unremitting effort. Historians write that he personally supervised the construction and made full use of all his empire could offer. The two most famous architects of the age, Anthemius of Tralles (Aydın) and Isidorus of Miletus, were entrusted with the construction of the building. They supervised one hundred master builders and ten thousand labourers.

The finest and rarest materials from the four corners of the empire were brought to Constantinople to be used in the construction of Hagia Sophia. The prophyry columns previously taken to Rome from an Egyptian temple in Heliopolis, ivory and gold icons, and ornaments from ancient temples in Ephesus, Kizikos and Baalbek were among them. The construction was completed in a very short time.

*Hagia Sophia in the 19th century. (from the Fossati album)*

It took five years, ten months and four days, from February 23rd 532 to December 27th 537. During the dedication ceremony, Emperor Justinian put aside formalities of state and entered the church excitedly, to say a prayer of thanks to God for allowing him to fulfill his dearest wish.

He cried with pride, remembering the temple in Jerusalem "Oh, Solomon, I have surpassed thee".

Later, the church was damaged many times by earthquakes and fires, and had to be repaired and reinforced.

On August 15th 553, January 14th 557 and May 7th 559, earthquakes destroyed the eastern side of the dome. The damage was repaired by the nephew of the original architect, Isidorus. He increased the height of the dome by 2.65 metres and built buttresses in the form of towers to support the dome.

On February 9th 869, during the reign of Emperor Basil I (867-886), an earthquake damaged the western side of the building. It was repaired in 870.

On October 25th 986, a violent earthquake resulted in the collapse of the western apse and caused partial damage to the dome. The church had to be closed until the architect Tridat finished repairing it in 994.

In 1204, the church was sacked by the Fourth Crusaders. During the Palaeologian age, Emperor Michael VIII (1261-1282) had

Hagia Sophia repaired by the architect Ruchas, and the buttresses in the south-west were added at that time.

In 1317, during the reign of Emperor Andronicus II, the north-eastern and south-western walls were reinforced on the exterior by pyramid-shaped buttresses.

In 1348, the eastern half of the dome collapsed and was afterwards repaired. In the first half of the 15th century, travellers and other sources described Hagia Sophia as being in a state of disrepair.

When the Turks conquered Constantinople in 1453, the church was converted into a mosque, a place of Islamic worship. To begin with, Turks preserved the frescoes and mosaic figures of Christian saints which decorated the walls. However, in the 16th century, these were completely covered by plaster, since the Islamic code forbids figural representation.

After it became a mosque, the following changes, necessitated by Islamic architectural standards, were made:

Sultan Mehmed II "the Conqueror" built an altar (mihrap) in the east,since the apse should be in the direction of Mecca and the brick minaret on the south-east corner of the edifice.

Sultan Bayezid (1484-1512) added a minaret on the north-east corner.

The Turkish architect Sinan, built the two minarets in front of the church during the reign of Sultan Murad III (1574-1595). Murad III also had water urns of the Hellenistic period (300 BC) brought to the mosque from Bergama.

The pulpit (minber) and preacher's pew (müezzin mahfili) were added to the interior during the reign of Murad IV.

In 1739, Sultan Mahmud I built a library and a primary school (mekteb-i sıbyan) in the south.

In 1850, Sultan Abdülmecit added the present day Imperial Pew. During his reign (1839-1861), important repairs were entrusted to the Swiss architect Gaspare Fossati. He removed the plaster covering the mosaics and then replastered them. He decorated these newly plastered areas with frescoes. The building was completely renovated inside and out. An horologion was built to the south of the structure.

In 1926, the government of the new Republic of Turkey, appointed a technical commission to investigate the architectural and static state of the building thoroughly. According to the commission's report, the foundation of the structure rested solidly on a bed of rock. Following Kemal Atatürk's orders, Hagia Sophia was converted into a museum on February 1st 1935. Atatürk visited the museum a few days later, on February 6th 1935.

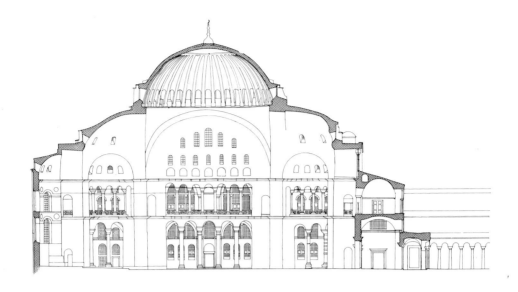

*Longitudinal section of Hagia Sophia.*

*Cross-section of Hagia Sophia.*

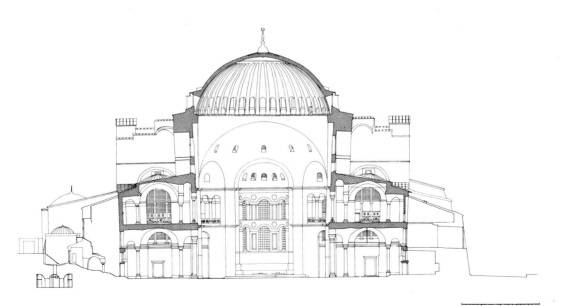

# VISITING HAGIA SOPHIA MUSEUM

T he entrance to the museum is at the front of the building. Before entering the museum, the ruins of the second Hagia Sophia found outside in front of the building, are worth seeing.

The excavations carried out in front and only to the left of the building, so as not to endanger it, unearthed the remains of the facade of Hagia Sophia built by Theodosius II. The steps and the door of the portico can be seen here, in the great hollow. The roofing material of the portico and other remains of the facade, are found both in the hollow, and in an area a few metres to the north. These architectural pieces bear the characteristics of the 5th century.

The facade of the building has been reconstructed with finds such as rafters, arches, alcoves, columns and capitals. Carved on the rafter seen in the hollow, is a scene of lambs which, according to Christian iconography, represent the believers. Undoubtedly, the rest of the scene is still buried. Excavations revealed mosaic decorations on the floor but these have been removed. Justinian's Hagia Sophia was built on top of these remains. The German professor A.M. Schneider carried out the excavations in 1936.

*Remains of the facade of the second Hagia Sophia.*

# THE EXONARTHEX

**A**s the doors of the entrance to Justinian's Hagia Sophia were added later, they are not of the decorated ancient Byzantine variety. The main entrance leads to the exonarthex which is 60.9 metres long and 6.03 metres wide, and its ceiling is covered with groined vaulting. During the Byzantine era, the exonarthex was reserved for those who had not yet been baptized. Doors to the minarets added in the Ottoman era, are found at the northern and southern ends.

Originally there were seven doors from the atrium to the exonarthex. Today, two of these are not used, and another two lead into rooms which were added later. Most of the archaeological treasures exhibited in the exonarthex are Byzantine objects found in various places in Istanbul. Among these are the three rows of plaster moulage of tablets upon which the decisions of the 1166 Council were inscribed. From the exonarthex there are five entrances to the inner narthex. The oak doors covered with bronze plates belong to the Byzantine era. The three middle doors have been cleaned recently, and it was found that once they were gilded. They are exquisitely decorated. The other two doors have been modified.

*Entrance to the exonarthex.*

15

# THE INNER NARTHEX

T he groined vaulted ceiling of the inner narthex is completely covered with mosaic, and the walls are of veined marble. The colourful mosaics of floral and geometric motifs on a gold background, create a magnificent appearance. The characteristics of Justinian's time are best preserved in the inner narthex. The cross motif is used throughout the mosaic design of the ceiling. As ancient sources indicate, during this period there were no figural mosaics. However, the figural mosaic decoration of the imperial door is a very important work of art. After it was uncovered and its discovery was published in 1933, its age and identification became the subject of debate for historians.

This scene depicts Jesus sitting on a magnificent celestial throne. His right hand is raised in a gesture of blessing, and in His left hand He holds an open book bearing the inscription: "Peace be with you. I am the Light of the World." On either side of Jesus, there are roundels. The one on the left portrays the Virgin Mary, and that on the right portrays the angel Gabriel. Jesus, potrayed here as the Pantocrator (King of the World), is dressed in white hiton and himation, and his features resemble Zeus, the king of gods.

*Details of the dome's mosaics.*

17

The latest research revealed that the bearded emperor prostrate on Jesus'lower left represents Emperor Leon VI. Although the scene is uncharacteristic of Byzantine iconography, the emperor is depicted imploring Chrits's forgiveness.

The subject of the scene is the three marriages of Leo VI, a situation contrary to the doctrine of the Orthodox church. Since the emperor was still without a male heir even after three marriages, he was allowed to marry his mistress Zoë, the mother of his illegitimate son, after a long dispute.

Thus, his son Porphyrogenitus became the legal heir to the throne. Emperor Constantine VII Porphyrogenitus is famous for his

*Columns and arcades of the Northern side.*

"Book of Ceremonies", which describes the religious ceremonies performed in Hagia Sophia. The mosaic is dated after the death of the emperor, around 920 AD.

The large door at the northern side of the inner narthex opens to the kochlias which leads to the upper gallery. The door on the south side opens into a vestibule, which leads to what has been the main entrance of the building since the 10th century.

There are nine doors leading from the narthex to the main halls. Of these, the three southern doors were used by the public, and those seeking sanctuary used the three northern doors. Although these doors are simply designed, the three middle doors used by the

*Mosaic above the Imperial Gate.*

emperor and his procession have elaborate decorations. The most impressive is the Imperial Gate in the centre. The sources indicate that, originally the doors were covered with gold and silver plates which were stripped off by the Fourth Crusaders. As a matter of fact, when the large door was cleaned, traces of gold were found. According to a legend, the doors were made of wood taken from Noah's Ark. None of the present doors are original.

Over the Imperial Gate there is a bronze cornice which has been the subject of many interesting legends. The scene in the middle of the cornice depicts a throne with an open book and a pigeon.

*North-West corner of the building.*

# THE GENERAL CHARACTERISTICS OF THE EDIFICE

T he Imperial Gate leads to the central nave of Hagia Sophia. The magnificent view created by the high dome, marble columns and arches is overwhelming. The dome is 55.6 metres high and approximately 31.36 metres wide. Due to repairs and earthquakes over the centuries, the large dome is not completely circular any more. The ceiling is completely covered with mosaics. The dome rests on four large arches, and these arches are supported by four pillars. Some of the weight of the dome is transmitted to the semi-domes in the north and south, and to the lower sections.

The interior of Hagia Sophia contains 107 columns. 40 of these are found on the ground floor and the rest are up in the gallery. Over the years, buttresses have been built outside, against almost every wall, to lessen the stress of the building and to counteract the damage caused by earthquakes.

As mentioned before, Hagia Sophia was built on a domed basilica plan. Accordingly, it has a central nave, northern and southern side naves, and two narthexes in the west. Only in the central nave is it possible to see all the way up to the dome. A second storey, the gallery, was built over the two side naves and the inner narthex. The distance from the Imperial Gate to the apse is 79.30 metres. The length of the edifice is approximately 100 metres. The width of the main nave is 32.27 metres and together with the side naves, the total width is 70 metres. From these measurements we conclude that Hagia Sophia covers an area of 7.500 square metres and is the fourth largest,as well as being the oldest church in the world after St. Peter's in Rome, Seville Cathedral and Milan Cathedral.

# THE DOME

T he dome is constructed of light bricks and its interior is covered with mosaics. Decorative mosaic bands radiate from the crown to the base of the dome. Documents indicate that the crown was previously decorated with a mosaic representation

*The dome and the pendentives.*

of Christ the Pantocrator.

Today, it is replaced by an inscription from the Koran which was created by Kazasker İzzet Efendi in the 19th century. The forty windows at the base of the dome are decorated with multicoloured mosaics. Four-winged cherubims are depicted in the pendentives.

The cherubims in the eastern pendentives are of mosaic, those in the western pendentives are frescoes. Since figural representations are against the Islamic code, the faces of the cherubims were covered with gold leaf medallions in the 19th century during the last major restoration.

# THE WALLS

 **N** umerous windows were built in the southern and northern walls to reduce the stress of the dome's weight transmitted to the walls by the arches. The walls are supported by pillars.

Mosaic figures of religious leaders dressed in white ceremonial gowns, with their names inscribed beside them, decorate the niches in the northern wall. From west to east: In the first niche is St. Ignatius, Patriarch of Constantinople, in the central niche, St. Chrysostom and in the third niche, St. Ignatius Theophorus, Patriarch of Antioch. All are dated the 10th century.

The walls of the main nave are covered with marble up to the upper reaches of the gallery. The walls of the side naves and inner narthex are covered with marble from floor to ceiling.

These valuable marbles of all colours from different regions of the empire, were specially selected for Hagia Sophia. It is said that the white marble from the Island of Marmara (Proconnenus), the green marble, from the Island of Eğriboz and Mount Tagetus near Isparta, the pink marble from Synada near Afyonkarahisar, the yellow marble from Africa and the red marble from North Africa, were all brought to Constantinople from those places. The veined marbles were cut symmetrically to create the decorative patterns which adorn the walls. Descriptive stone carvings in special panel form are found mostly in the two side naves. Some of these are found above the Imperial Gate on the inside. Around the decorative roundels on the left and right, dolphins are depicted, and among them is the trident of

*Columns supporting the lateral walls.*

*Decorative marble panels on the walls.*

*Mosaics of St. Chrysostome.*

Poseidon. Over these two panels is an ornament in the shape of a temple.

A cross is seen behind the curtain between the columns. After the church was converted into a mosque, panels with inscriptions from the Koran were placed in certain parts of the buildings. Until the 19th century, huge panels mounted at the level of the gallery were hung from the piers. When these deteriorated, they were replaced by medallions 7.5 metres in diameter during the reign of Sultan Abdülmecid, and inscribed by the famous calligrapher, Kazasker Mustafa İzzet Efendi, with the words: "Allah", "Muhammed", the names of the first caliph, and Caliph Ali's sons, Hasan and Hüseyin.

*A mosaic cross motif and details of the marble covered wall.*

# THE APSE

T he semi-dome of the apse is completely covered with mosaics. When the plaster was removed in 1935, a mosaic depicting the Virgin Mary holding the Christ-child in her lap was discovered. Two angels also appear in the scene. The archangel

*Imperial Pew.*

Michael, depicted in the north, is almost totally destroyed, only his feet remain. The archangel Gabriel, standing on the right holding a globe in his left hand and a staff in his right, is also damaged.

Figures are imposed on a gold mosaic background. The figure of the Virgin Mary is still in perfect condition. She is wearing a green cloak and sitting on a jewelled throne. The Christ-child is wearing a golden cloak and has a very mature expression on His face. This mosaic panel is dated to the 9th century.

*One of the marble jars of the Hellenistic age.*

On the face of the apse conch is a damaged inscription in Greek. Not much is known about the decoration of the large windows in the apse during the Byzantine era. The present stained-glass windows have 19th century Turkish designs.

The upper parts of the arches connecting the windows, are decorated with engraved calligraphy and small disc panels inscribed with the words "Allah", "Muhammed", and the names of the caliphs. These decorations are in total harmony with the rest of the architectural ornamentation. Since the apse does not face Mecca, Islamic architects added an altar facing south, after Hagia Sophia became a mosque. An inscription from the Koran is seen on the frieze of blue tiles. The frieze extends all along the apse.

The bronze candelabras in front of the altar were brought from Hungary by Kanuni Sultan Süleyman (Süleyman the Magnificent) and presented to Hagia Sophia. The areas on either side of the apse are covered with decorative Turkish tiles. That to the north was converted into an imperial tribune by the addition of a floor. It was decorated with tiles and a small altar was added. It was used by the sultans until Mahmud II (1808-1839), and later a magnificent pew was erected on the same side. The entrance to the pew seen today, is through a separate door in the east, in front of the Sultan Ahmed III Fountain built in the 19th century. Its ornamentation and architecture exhibit the characteristics of Turkish, Byzantine and European baroque art.

*Columns and arcades of the gallery.*

*A view of the gallery.*

# COLUMNS AND CAPITALS

U ndoubtedly, the columns, capitals, and the arches connecting them, are important elements enriching the architectural beauty of Hagia Sophia. We may even say that the masterpieces of the 6th century art of carving are to be found here. The column heads are meticulously carved in exquisite lace-like designs.

The monograms of Justinian and his wife Theodora can also be seen on the column capitals. The carving on the arches connecting the columns display the same quality of work. The lower sections of the arches are decorated with mosaics, and the exterior surfaces are ornamented in "opus sectile".

The most important of Hagia Sophia's 107 columns are located on the ground floor. Some of these were brought from ancient temples and monuments in different regions of the empire.

Historical sources agree that they were acquired from the Temple of the Sun god Heliopolis, from the Temple of Artemis in Ephesus, and from monuments in Rome and Baalbek. Yet, the measurements of these columns do not match the size of the temples from which they are supposed to have come (for example, the Temple of Artemis in Ephesus). It is certain that there are columns in Hagia Sophia acquired from ancient monuments. There are also columns which were carved especially for Hagia Sophia in Thessaly and the Island of Marmara (Proconnesus).

*A spot adorned with gallery columns and arcades.*

Black-veined, grey marble from the Island of Marmara was also used to pave the floor. Large blocks of marble were sawn into plates, and these were fitted in such a way that the natural veins of the marble were connected.

*Capital with monogram.*

*Some of the columns and arches.*

# THE SOUTHERN NAVE

T he ceiling of the southern nave is covered with 6th century gold mosaics, and the vaults and arches are decorated with multicoloured geometric and floral designs. The cross motifs may still be seen through the varnish they were covered with in the 19th century. Decorative panels embellish the marble vaults. The two panels facing each other on the eastern side are decorated with Poseidon's trident and dolphins, which were a coat of arms in Byzantine times.

Next to these, in the south-eastern end of the church, stands a rectangular column on which there is a hand print. There were many legends about this hand print. As the sources indicate, this piece of stone was added later onto the column. It was originally found in the Theotokos Church at Ayvansaray and the hand print was accepted as the Virgin Mary's. When the church burned down, the stone was brought to Hagia Sophia.

The area right in front of the library, between the columns and the pillar, was known as the Metatorium. The emperor watched the religious ceremonies from here.

*Decorative bronze door of the library.*

# OTTOMAN LIBRARY

**O**ne of the most beautiful buildings of the Ottoman period, it was built during the reign of Sultan Mahmud I (1739). It is built between two buttresses. Viewed from the inside, it enhances rather than spoils the general architectural style. The main section where the books are stored and the reading room, are decorated with the most famous ancient Turkish tiles.

There are tiles from İznik, Kütahya, Tekfur Palace, and even a few from Europe. The engraved wood bookshelves have a characteristic form, and historical objects pertaining to the library are displayed here.

*Details of the mosaics on the arches in the nave. The motifs on the crosses belong to the 19th century.*

# THE MAIN NAVE

**T**he floor of the main nave is covered with grey and white marble. The square area in the pavement next to the preacher's pulpit is decorated with square and circular slabs of marble. According to some sources, the emperors were crowned here (13th century). This type of flooring is foreign to Hagia Sophia's architectural style. Therefore, it was probably brought here from another monument. In general, the emperors were crowned on the ambon in the middle of the church.

The preacher's pulpit and smaller pews were placed in such a way that they do not upset the general architectural effect.

The two huge Hellenistic urns on either side of the Imperial Gate were brought from the ancient ruins in Bergama. According to a rumour, they were presented to Hagia Sophia by Sultan Murad III. During the Ottoman period, each was fitted with a lid and a faucet and used for ablutions.

*Western gallery.*

# THE NORTHERN SIDE NAVE

T he decoration of the ceiling and walls are similar to those of the southern nave. The wall panels depict different themes. Near the door to the narthex is a rectangular pillar, the lower section of which is covered with a brass plate bearing a hole. It is the subject of many legends and is known as the "sweating cloumn". In Byzantine times, it was referred to as "St. Gregory's Miracle Column". It attracts the most attention in Hagia Sophia.

Visitors stick their fingers in the hole and make a wish which they think will come true if their finger comes out wet. Some believe that the moisture cures eye diseases. In reality, the column is of the type of stone which absorbs moisture easily. The hole is just coincidental.

*Figure of Virgin Mary in deesis.*

*Figure of St. John the Baptist in deesis.*

# THE GALLERY

T he most recent work done in uncovering the mosaics, revealed a figural mosaic in the gallery. An inclined kochlias leads to the upper gallery from the northern side of the narthex. Actually, there is a kochlias in each of the four corners of the edifice leading to the upper gallery, but the one on the south-eastern side was closed by the buttress and minaret built later.

The church has three galleries: the northern, southern and western galleries. Historical documents indicate that, the western gallery was the most important one, since it was reserved for the empress and her retinue. According to the same sources, the northern gallery was used as a gynaeceum reserved for women. In the centre of the western gallery, which was reserved for the emperor's family, there is a square area surrounded by mosaics of "opus sectile" work.

A circular green piece of marble from Thessaly can be seen to the east of this square area, which was reserved for the empress and her retinue to observe religious ceremonies.

The vault of the gallery today is devoid of decorations, but most probably it was covered with mosaics during the Byzantine era.

As one enters the southern gallery, the most attractive one today, one faces a marble partition resembling an antique bronze door in style. Research revealed that this partition is not contemporary with the church but was placed here later, its magnificence being due to the fact that the area behind it was used for a very important function. The area was actually reserved for countcil meetings and was known as the Council Hall. It was called "the Gate to Heaven and Hell" by the people.

On the eastern wall, immediately south of the apse, there is a mosaic panel depicting Jesus Christ, Empress Zoë and Emperor Constantine IX. Monomachus, Jesus Christ, seated on a throne, is holding the Bible in His left hand while His right hand is lifted in blessing. On His right, the emperor is offering a money-bag, and on His left, the empress is holding a scroll in her hands. The words "Sovereign of the Romans, Constantine Monomachus" are inscribed

*Jesus Christ, with Emperor Constantine IX Monomachus on the left and Empress Zoë on the right.*

*Alexius.*

above his head. The inscription above the head of the empress reads "Zoë, the most pious Augusta". In this 11th century mosaic, both the emperor and the empress are wearing their ceremonial garments. It is said that on the occasion of each of Zoë's three marriages, the face of the previous emperor was replaced by that of the new one.

*Head of Empress Eirene.*

*Emperor John II Comnenus, the Virgin Mary holding the Christ-child and Empress Eirene.*

The mosaic to the right of the window depicts the Virgin Mary holding the Chirst-child, Emperor John II Comn enus (1118-1143), and his wife, Empress Eirene, daughter of King Ladislaus I of Hungary. The portrait of Prince Alexius is seen on an extension of the wall. Both the emperor and his wife were famous for being devoutly religious and charitable. Devoid of the stiffness apparent in portraits of sovereigns, both the emperor and the empress are depicted in this 12th century mosaic with the soft, realistic expressions befitting their character.

Turning back and looking west, one faces a mosaic panel which is considered one of the most magnificent mosaics of Byzantium: the Deësis. Unfortunately, the lower section of the mosaic has been damaged. Christ is portrayed in the centre with St. John the Baptist on His right and the Virgin Mary on His left. The expression on their faces is very realistic and appropriate with the theme of Deësis.

The compassionate expression of Christ, and the look of entreaty of the other two, are very expressive. Although its exact date is a matter of dispute, the mosaic belongs, probably, to the first half of the 12th century. It demonstrates the same technique as that used in the mosaics of the Church of Chora.

At the base of the wall opposite the Deësis, is a stone tablet on which the name Hericus Dandalo is inscribed. Dandalo, Doge of Venice, came to Constantinople with the Fourth Crusade and caused much vandalism. It is claimed that he is buried at this spot.

Before leaving this section, the frescoes by Fossati on the ceiling of the dome attract the attention. These are 19th century copies of ancient mosaic motifs. From Fossati's records and illustrations, we may conclude that there are figural mosaics under the plaster on the vaults. The results of exploratory work carried on in recent years prove this.

*Mosaics which are still covered with plaster.*

The same supposition may be made about the vaults in the northern gallery. Here too, the frescoes were done by Fossati in the 19th century. In recent years, a mosaic depicting Emperor Alexander standing, was discovered in the northern gallery. He reigned with his brother Leon VI. The fact that his mosaic portrait is in such a dark and forgotten corner, seems to be a reference to his weak character. In the galleries, there are other well preserved mosaics of floral motifs on the soffits of the arches between the columns. These are contemporary with the church. In the rooms located at the southern end of the western gallery, there are 6th century decorative mosaics as well as descriptive mosaics belonging to later periods; they are badly damaged. These rooms during the Byzantine era, were reserved for the church leaders.

# THE EXIT

As one descends to the narthex from the gallery and looks back before leaving the southern vestibule, one sees an exquisite mosaic in the tympanum, above the door. The Virgin Mary is depicted sitting on a jewelled throne, holding the Christ-child on her knees. Two emperors on either side of her are holding objects in their hands. On her left, Emperor Constantine is offering her a model of Constantinople, and on her right, Emperor Justinian is offering her a model of Hagia Sophia. Both emperors are wearing their impressive ceremonial gowns. Uncovered in 1933, the mosaic has a gold background. There are monograms in the roundels on either side of Mary's head and the Christ-child has a mature expression on His face. The inscription next to Justinian reads from top to bottom, "Glorious Monarch Justinian", and the one next to Constantine reads, "Saintly Constantine, Great Sovereign". This descriptive mosaic panel belongs to the last half of the 10th century.

The ceiling of the vestibule is decorated with geometric and floral mosaic motifs. The damaged areas of these mosaics were repaired and finished with frescoes.

This entrance hall, called the "Vestibule of the Warriors" in the Book of Ceremonies, occupies an important place in the history of Hagia Sophia. When the main (western) entrance could not be used for some reason (through damage by earthquakes etc.) after the 10th or 9th centuries, this southern vestibule was used more frequently. Both the mosaic above the entrance, and the bronze door which opens outwards support this theory. The bronze door, dated to the 1st century BC, was brought to Hagia Sophia from a Hellenistic temple in Tarsus and is considered the most splendid door of the church.

It has great historical and artistic value. It was placed in the church in the 9th century by Emperor Theophilus, and the date 838 is engraved on it. Later, different emperors had their monograms engraved on the door. During the Byzantine era, it was known as the "Glorious Entrance". Thus, we conclude that entrance into Hagia Sophia changed in the 9th century.

The door from the vestibule to the horologion in the east is closed for use, today. The sources indicate that, in the horologion there was a suite where the emperors changed costumes and also a water clock.

*Details of the mosaic showing Emperor Constantine.*

# SUBSIDIARY BUILDINGS OF HAGIA SOPHIA

D ifferent sources mention three separate annexes to the main building, two of which, the Skevophylakion (the Treasury) and the Baptisterion (the Baptistry) still stand. The third was the Patriarchate, which was built along the southern wall of the church. None of its ruins have remained.

The Treasury, recently excavated by this author, is a circular building north-east of Hagia Sophia. The buttresses built around it have completely separated it from the church. During the Ottoman era, a door was added on the northern side to allow its use as a provisions depot for the church. During the Byzantine era, sacred relics were stored and holy bread and wine were prepared here.

The Baptistry, on the right of Hagia Sophia's main entrance, was the most important baptistry in Byzantium. The building is square on the outside and octagonal on the inside, and it has a narthex on its western side. After the church was converted into a mosque, the baptistry was used to store the oils for the oil lamps (Kandil) of the mosque. Later, the colossal marble container for the baptismal was moved to the northern courtyard, and the baptistry was converted into a mausoleum. Sultan Mustafa I and Sultan İbrahim were buried here.

# SUBSIDIARY ISLAMIC BUILDINGS

A fter Hagia Sophia was converted into a mosque, as in the case with other large mosques, many religious and secular buildings were constructed in its vicinity according to Turkish-Islamic tradition. The Medrese (theological school), İmaret (charity organisation), Çeşme (fountain), Hamam (public bath) were just a few of them. Since this was the most important mosque, many sultans were buried in the mausoleums in its surrounds.

## THE FOUNTAIN (ŞADIRVAN)

I n the stone courtyard, the first Turkish monument which catches the eye, is the impressive fountain for ablutions (Şadırvan). Built to serve as a place for ritual ablutions before praying, it is a superb example of Ottoman baroque art. It was built by Sultan Mahmud I in 1740. Next to the fountain is the primary school (Sıbyan Mektebi) built by the same sultan.

On the left of the exit is a building now used as an office. Built in the 19th century, it was once the "Muvakkithane" (the clock room). In the middle of the room, on a round table, once stood a large, extremely precise clock. The pupils could look through the windows to find out the exact time.

North of Hagia Sophia, there were two important edifices built during the Turkish era: the Medrese (theological school) and the İmaret (charity organisation). The Medrese has been totally demo-

*Şadırvan (the fountain).*

lished in recent years, but the İmaret is in good condition and serves as a depot. Built by Sultan Murad III in the 16th century, it was used to distribute food to the needy.

The Hamam (public bath) is 100 metres from Hagia Sophia, situated to the east of Sultanahmet Park.

# THE MAUSOLEUMS

**A**ll of the four mausoleums were built to the south of Hagia Sophia. The baptistry was also converted into a mausoleum. The facade of each mausoleum is decorated with ornamental tiles and exquisitely crafted doors.

The first small building, in the section of the courtyard where the mausoleums are located, is a mausoleum of the crown princes.

The second is that of Sultan Murad III (1546-1595). A total of fifty-four sultannas and crown princes repose in this mausoleum built by the famous architect Davut Ağa.

The third mausoleum is that of Sultan Selim II. It was built in the 16th century by the most famous of all Turkish architects, Sinan, and is an exquisite example of Islamic architecture. It has an overwhelming atmosphere of serenity. Covered with richly patterned tiles, masterpieces of wood carving and calligraphy decorate the walls.

Sultan Mehmed III (1595-1603) lies in the next mausoleum. Some of the crown princes of the same family and the women of the palace, also rest in this same mausoleum.

*The door of the mauseleum.*

*Tile panel at the entrance of the mausoleum of Murad III. (16th century)*

# PUBLICATION LIST

**TURKEY (BN)** *(In English, French, German, Italian, Spanish, Dutch)*
**ANCIENT CIVILIZATIONS AND RUINS OF TURKEY** *(In English)*
**ISTANBUL (B)** *(In English, French, German, Italian, Spanish, Japanese)*
**ISTANBUL (ORT)** *(In English, French, German, Italian, Spanish)*
**ISTANBUL (BN)** *(In English, French, German, Italian, Spanish, Japanese)*
**MAJESTIC ISTANBUL** *(In English, German)*
**TURKISH CARPETS** *(In English, French, German, Italian, Spanish, Japanese)*
**TURKISH CARPETS** *(In English, German)*
**THE TOPKAPI PALACE** *(In English, French, German, Italian, Italian, Spanish, Japanese, Turkish)*
**HAGIA SOPHIA** *(In English, French, German, Italian, Spanish)*
**THE KARİYE MUSEUM** *(In English, French, German, Italian, Spanish)*
**ANKARA** *(In English, French, German, Italian, Spanish, Turkish)*
**Unique CAPPADOCIA** *(In English, French, German, Italian, Spanish, Japanese, Turkish)*
**CAPPADOCIA (BN)** *(In English, French, German, Italian, Spanish, Dutch, Turkish)*
**EPHESUS** *(In English, French, German, Italian, Spanish, Japanese)*
**EPHESUS (BN)** *(In English, French, German, Italian, Spanish, Dutch)*
**APHRODISIAS** *(In English, French, German, Italian, Spanish, Turkish)*
**THE TURQUOISE COAST OF TURKEY** *(In English)*
**PAMUKKALE (HIERAPOLIS)** *(In English, French, German, Italian, Spanish, Dutch, Japanese, Turkish)*
**PAMUKKALE (BN)** *(In English, French, German, Italian, Spanish)*
**PERGAMON** *(In English, French, German, Italian, Spanish, Japanese)*
**LYCIA (AT)** *(In English, French, German)*
**KARIA (AT)** *(In English, French, German)*
**ANTALYA (BN)** *(In English, French, German, Italian, Dutch, Turkish)*
**PERGE** *(In English, French, German)*
**ASPENDOS** *(In English, French, German)*
**ALANYA** *(In English, French, German, Turkish)*
**The Capital of Urartu: VAN** *(In English, French, German)*
**TRABZON** *(In English, French, German, Turkish)*
**TURKISH COOKERY** *(In English, French, German, Italian, Spanish, Dutch, Japanese, Turkish)*
**NASREDDİN HODJA** *(In English, French, German, Italian, Spanish, Japanese)*
**TÜRKÇE-JAPONCA KONUŞMA KILAVUZU** *(Japanese-Turkish)*
**ANADOLU UYGARLIKLARI** *(Turkish)*

## MAPS

**TURKEY (NET), TURKEY (ESR), TURKEY (WEST)**
**TURKEY (SOUTH WEST), ISTANBUL, MARMARİS,**
**ANTALYA-ALANYA, ANKARA, İZMİR, CAPPADOCIA**

## NET® BOOKSTORES

ISTANBUL
Galleria Ataköy, Sahil Yolu, 34710 Ataköy - Tel: (9-1) 559 09 50
Ramada Hotel, Ordu Caddesi, 226, 34470 Laleli - Tel: (9-1) 513 64 31
İZMİR
Cumhuriyet Bulvarı, 142/B, 35210 Alsancak - Tel: (9-51) 21 26 32